To Berenice,

May living loved, heavenly encounters and hearing God's voice be part of your life style. Heaven knows and adores you.

Love Ngo xx

LIVING LOVED

EXPERIENCE THE NATURE OF GOD AS LOVE

NQO MAFUKIDZE

LIVING LOVED

EXPERIENCE THE NATURE OF GOD AS LOVE

GOD IS LOVE

COVER DESIGN: Tinashe Saruchera

EDIT & TYPESET: Brad Odilo

For more information: **www.nqomafukidze.com**

ISBN: 978-0-6397-4365-3

Published in the United Kingdom

Endorsements

"Nqo is a powerful voice with an incredibly grounded testimony in the truth of Jesus Christ and His love. Anyone who reads the words contained in this book, that were formed through experience with the truth of God's love will find freedom and wholeness."

ALTON EUGENE aka ALTON KIING
Billboard, Dove Award and 3 time Grammy Winner, Musician, Songwriter, Producer, Singer, Founding Member of Maverick City Music, USA

"Nqo is a gifted communicator and an anointed minister who walks in signs, wonders and deliverance. She carries a brilliant display of knowing what it is to be a daughter of God. Her book "Living Loved" is nothing short of that. Nqo carries a profound revelation of living in His love in any and all seasons. Through reading her book each reader will be marked with not only fresh understanding, but a deeper encounter with the love of God. Get ready to be transformed by the testimony of Christ in her life!"

BENJAMIN ARMSTRONG
Senior Leader and Director of Prophetic Ministries at Bethel Church, Redding California, USA

"A mind-renewing deep dive into the love of Father God. "Living Loved" isn't only a repetition of the author's experience, but an ever-increasing invitation into creating your own marked moments with God's love in every chapter. If you've ever had trouble getting your head-knowledge of God's love into a place where you can feel it at a heart-level, this guided tour through scripture, story, declaration, and listening prayer will help you complete that journey of head to heart. Enjoy being led into a greater measure of the revelation of the mystery of our adoption into Christ and His Kingdom, and prepare to realise afresh that you are the apple of His eye."

CARISA DOWNS

Worship Leader, Author of Softer God: Poems and Divine Conversations and I Can Hear You, Little Rock, Arkansas, USA

"With this revelation of Living Loved, Nqo represents the rapidly emerging generation of prophetic voices to the Body of Christ. According to the scriptures, our faith is activated by love. Your faith and hope will be bolstered as you study this fresh manna. There is power in the words inscribed in this book. When a fuller understanding of love is engrafted in the spirit (heart), partiality, limitation and inability to access new realms is done away with. This results in the manifestation of and the completeness of the richest measures of God's power and presence embedded in you (Ephesians 3:19). When I look at the cross, it's more than a crucifixion. I see love manifest. The Apostle Paul says, Jesus loved me and gave Himself up for me (Galatians 2:20). As you read Living Loved, this revelation will be engrafted in your spirit and heart and cause you to access new realms in God. Enjoy Living Loved!"

CONRAD SSEKKOBA

Psalmist, Youth Pastor and Leader, Fields of Harvest Ministries, Miracle Centre Cathedral, Kampala, Uganda

"In this hurting world, it's essential that the church understands love within the perimeter of God's word. Nqo has paid the price to give us this highly significant and informative book. This is a message from the mind and heart of God. When you prayerfully read this book you will come to the same conclusion Nqo has, God is love. I look forward to seeing a great Kingdom gain through widespread distribution of this book."

PASTOR DAN OMBIJA
Pastor of Hopewell Christian Fellowship Church Kilgoris, Kenya, Director of Mission Team for Christ International The Missionary Church East Africa Coordinator

"'Living Loved' is a book that is soaked in the simple, empowering, and overwhelming love of God. Nqo's personal stories and Biblical examples of how God's love wrecked her life are inspiring and life changing. I have personally known Nqo for the last few years, and have been impacted by her zeal for the reality of the Gospel to touch people's lives. What she has written in this book aren't just good thoughts shared for people to read. They are actual testimonies from her own experience with Jesus which are honest and real. I am thankful to have had her testimonies reach my life and I am excited to see them touch yours as well. As you read Living Loved, I believe the impartation that flows from the Holy Spirit that was given to Nqo is going to impact your life. You will never be the same! Enjoy being loved."

DARRIOUS WILLIAMSON
Leader at Bethel School of Supernatural Ministry Bethel Church, Redding CA, USA

"After 12 years of full time ministry, in 2014 I encountered a wonderfully unique, warm, red-haired, God-loving girl who talked in a way I had not experienced before. She used words like 'daddy' when she prayed and talked terrifyingly openly to me about the depth of God's love. Once I got past the huge initial annoyance and embarrassment that the use of this 'soppy' language caused a proud Geordie like me, we have become dear friends! Ministering together since, God has used Nqo's words and weekly fellowship to soften my heart, give a greater understanding of His love and allow the Holy Spirit to continue to shape the increasingly more rounded and whole version of myself that I am today. I encourage you to put aside any hardness of heart, deeply digest Nqo's exploration and unpacking of scripture and to 'Live Loved'."

DEZ MINTO
YFriday, EMI (2000 - 2010), Worship Pastor, Pastoral Ministries Rediscover Church, Exeter Elim Pentecostal Movement UK

"We are amazed and excited to see Nqo's ministry message take form in this book. Over the years, her dedication to serving God and His people have touched many hearts and souls across the globe. We ministered together in the most remote villages of Kenya and truly her life resonates this very message. In her book, Living Loved, Pastor Nqo articulately gives a clear impression of God, His kind of love, how it is expressed to mankind and how He expects us to receive and share the same on earth. We invite you to be a partaker of this liberating truth about God's love and how to live it."

REVEREND ELIJAH & PASTOR MERCY OSERAH
MTh Pastors of Global Revival Fire Ministries, The Solution Place, Nairobi, Kenya

"What a refreshing book at such a time as this. What makes it more powerful is that Nqo is the perfect example of the love of God personified. You cannot encounter her and not encounter the love of God. What I love about Living Loved is that it challenges religiousness and moves us into experiencing God's nature of Love. For me, the reminder that hit home is that 'I am not an orphan!' As someone who lost both parents there is the thinking that I am alone and without parental cover and yet, that is a lie because I do have a Father who loves me unconditionally. It brought tears to my eyes, not of sorrow but of joy. As you read this book, prepare to encounter the undiluted love of God, not just through words but through each Activation at the end of each chapter."

PASTOR EMELDA VHIRIRI-MAHACHI
Pastor of Prayer Fellowship Zimbabwe, Award Winning Development Practitioner, Worshipper, Author of From One Invaluable Woman to Another and Beauty for my Ashes: Rising Like a Phoenix From the Ashes of Grief, Founder of the Invaluable Women Exhale Community and Cultiv8 Africa

"If you open your heart and allow God to speak to you as you read this book, the message of Living Loved will really transform your life. A biblically foundational truth of a love that surpasses all. In a very practical and genuine way Nqo has laid out the truths of who God is, love. This is a truth we all know, but too often do not stop to let this truth go deep in our hearts. Read this book with the Holy Spirit, I guarantee somewhere in these pages God's love for you will touch you deeply. Beautifully written with a simple but powerful activation after every chapter that will refresh you and awaken your heart to Love. If you are struggling with the truth that Jesus loves you, I pray that this book will make it a reality for you as Nqo's exciting blend of truths and testimonies are revealed. I know Nqo personally lives this message of Living Loved and it is an invitation for the church to step into and open up to God because it is possible to Live Loved."

ESTHER BECKLEY
Founder of Crowns of Fire Ministries, UK

"This is a raw book about God's love that opens up a new way to be real with God. As you read it, deeper revelation of God's nature and His unconditional love will shape your perspective allowing you to have an intimate relationship with God. You can walk and live in love already because Jesus died for our sins, failures, mistakes and regrets. You don't have to wait any longer to enter such hopeful new creation life in Him and to experience what He promised you - unfailing love. I love how this book is also very practical with activations after each chapter, breaking lies in a very timely and prophetic manor and replacing them with truths on how God sees us. The author is so generous and vulnerable in opening up her journey to discovering this love of God as a daughter, as a wife and friend. It is powerful and inspiring. This book will lead you to a transformational lifestyle with God; to live loved."

ESTHER D. MORISHITA
Co-Founder of Awakening Asia, Co-Pastor of Awakening Tokyo Church, Japan Founder and Designer - Holy Nation Jewellery Brand

"Living Loved! Did you know that yielding to Holy Spirit also meant that He could inspire and write through a yielded vessel? I believe that every page in this treasure was written by author Nokunqoba Mafukidze and that Holy Spirit was holding the pen. This book is an invitation to embark on a new journey, of making or remaking a love history with God. It will take you through a process of freedom, activation, a fresh baptism of the fiery love of God and revive you to carry His love everywhere you go; to see other lives transformed."

FRIDA ISHIMWE
Evangelist, Speaker, Brussels, Belgium

"Nqo has written a book about one of the most important themes in all of Christianity, that is, how to experience God's love, and how to live in God's love in everyday circumstances, even in the hardest times. She expresses thoughts and situations that every Christian can identify with, explains how to get rid of demonic fear and shame, and live abundantly in God's love instead. Her writing is biblically based and her message is powerful: God knows you and loves you fully. At the end of every chapter, you will find practical instructions on how to activate the truth of God's love for you."

GORAN MEDVED
mag. theol.,
Bible Translator and New Testament Lecturer in Croatia

"This is great small book on the biggest truth of all - God is love. It is rooted in sound biblical theology. Even more, this book is a call to biblical practice, because God's love is not an abstract theory but experiential reality. And Nqo Mafukidze is showing us "how" and "why". Do Yourself a favor, read this beautiful book and step into freedom that God by His Love intended for You. Thank you Nqo for this eloquent exposé of the most needed truth that contemporary Church needs."

GORAN PUNDA
Pastor, Evangelical Pentecostal Church "Jelenovac", Zagreb, Croatia, Member of Presbytery EPCRH.

"In her book Living Loved, the Bona fide, impassioned Nqo Mafukidze construes in depth what it means to be loved by God. She richly interrogates line by line the wealth we have through the nature of God Himself being Love. She alludes that by deep intimacy with Him, we are able to live a life that evinces the benefits thereof. As I read through it I found myself in tears of joy as I got to understand deeper what it means to be loved by God. It has been one of my BEST reads. I encourage everyone created by God to purchase, partake and become all that God purposed you to be."

PASTOR GRACE KAPSWARA
International Speaker,
Pastor of Love City Church, Harare, Zimbabwe

"A dilapidated green sofa. This was one of the locations that I recall when I think of Nqo's journey to Living Loved. What is so precious about Living Loved is that this isn't an idea or a theological theory, this journey has been walked, cried through, and celebrated over. I can testify to that. Having known Nqo for over ten years, this fiery and powerful woman of God, has walked every inch of road that this book goes through. Not only will Living Loved give you an empowering and revolutionary picture of God's love, but it is also as genuine as they come. I have seen this journey change and transform Nqo and I have no doubt it will change and transform you. The Bible tells us 'the greatest of these is love,' and Living Loved beautifully articulates how to walk this great journey."

HANNAH BVUMBURA

Elder at Rediscover Church, Exeter, Elim Pentecostal Movement, UK, Speaker, Founder of The Me Project UK Charity

"This beautifully written book will cast out fear and override shame. It will enable you to walk out your life in love and extend the Father's heart to all people. Let it do its job in you. You will live in a more generous and fulfilled way. This is an excellent resource for small groups, married couples or singles, with the One called Love. This is a love challenge; a call to walk like Jesus. Knowing Nqo and watching her life, I can safely endorse the words of this book as being walked out authentically by the author. Nqo is a hug from heaven! We could do with more of this love released through our nation and I believe this book is a great catalyst for such a time as this."

HELEN YOUSAF

Prophetic Psalmist and Artist

Ordained Minister within the Elim Pentecostal Movement UK

"The call to live loved is a call from The Father and Nqo faithfully unpacks it in this book. She calls God's people to live with the radical realisation that we are loved and cherished beyond belief. And as such, we need not be dismayed, we need not cower in fear, and we need not shrink in shame for Christ's love emboldens us. Nqo is one who knows without a doubt she is beloved, thus writes with conviction, courage and compassion, that we may know the depths of His great love too."

IFY ALEXIS LEE
Christian Therapist & Minister, Founder of Love Limitless

"Living Loved is an eye opener, a perfect assurance of how deeply and intimately our heavenly Father loves us and that it is possible to walk in and enjoy His love. In an era filled with a lot of uncertainties, brokenness, low self-esteem, rejection and insecurities, Nqo transparently and beautifully leaves no stone unturned while inviting you to embrace our Father's love. She also invites you to believe that His Love is for you and that the Father in His Majestic splendour desires for you to see yourself the same way He sees you, loved. I truly believe that this book is life-changing and the message of God's unconditional, unfathomable love it carries will take the scales off your eyes and equip you with boldness and confidence to approach the throne of God; He is your loving Father."

JACQUELINE NALUGEMWA
Speaker, Hospitality Minister
Miracle Centre Cathedral, Kampala Uganda

"What a mesmerising time reading through the pages of this book in which love is not just a 4-letter word, but a true reality and experience of Nqo. With every letter, comma, and full-stop, one can feel the love of the Father oozing out of the text. Living Loved awakens one to the core reason of our existence, it takes us back to the cross, back to Love. Ephesians 3:18 AMP. To be fully capable of comprehending with all saints (God's people) the width, length, height and depth of His Love, full experience of that amazing and endless love."

PROPHETESS LIBA UNDI
Co-Pastor of Beloved Sons Ministries and Church South Africa.
Founder of She is Virtuous, Healing is Now, Lovers Night
Director and Co-Founder of Grace Care Foundation

"In a world where many live from fear, Nqo encourages us in this book to live loved. Shame, guilt and lies about our identity have warped our view of how deeply loved we are. With powerful declarations at the end of each chapter, I believe that if you take these truths seriously it will change the way that you live, walk and serve the world around you. It's time to live loved!"

DR LISA ADJEI
Founder of Sankofa Collective, Speaker
British Church Relations Manager for Christian Aid
Member of Racial Justice Working Group by CTE
Trustee at Churches Together England

""I was mistaken about an attribute of His nature that is the essence of who He is and it hurt His heart. He didn't just want my works, my Christian activity, or my spiritual gymnastics. The sobering truth was He wanted me. That's all. He is not in this for what we can do for Him. He is not in this for what you can achieve for Him. He is in this for you."
— Nqo Mafukidze

I've known Nqo for just over two years, yet in that short time, listening to her teach and speak has altered my long standing understanding of God's love for me. She embodies the message she has written in this book. She ensures that those she encounters not only experience but truly understand God's amazing love. She has a gentle, persistent, very effective way of driving home the message that empowers people to realise that they are loved, fully, completely and unconditionally by the Heavenly Father. Nothing is more liberating (from internal quarrels), enlightening (in moments of darkness and confusion), and inspiring (in moments of weakness or hopelessness) than this simple but deep understanding. It took me from cycles of highs and lows, confidence and condemnation, wins and mistakes; to a place of constant security and rest, unwavering trust and unending desire to do my best to love back the Lord who first loved me, and know that no matter how feeble, He is pleased by my every effort. I no longer turn away but rather lean into Him when I am weak, disappointed in myself and afraid that He may be disappointed with me. This is because I am learning to Live Loved."

LISA CHIRISERI

Pastor at His Presence Ministries International, Harare, Zimbabwe, Speaker, Zimbabwe's Top 40 under 30 Emerging Leaders 2015, Founder of FACEZ Education-Fund and Women in Energy Group, Top Ten African Youth in Philanthropy - African-Grantmakers-Network 2015

"Love is the source of all creation and He is the environment in which all of creation functions optimally. I'm afraid none of us are ever fully alive until we're living loved. I am so glad that Nqo has written this practical, spirit-filled guide to doing so. In it, she offers a refreshing challenge to awaken our hearts and minds to a tangible and pervasive experience of God's love. It's incredible to know that we can get to where it's no longer simply a place we visit, but the consciousness of His love becomes our permanent abode. I've had the privilege of watching the author live this truth out through life's peaks and valleys. Everything she shares is drawn directly from God's word and her own life. This revelation will undoubtedly break off the chains of shame and fear that have for so long held God's people captive!"

LUSANDA THWALA
Speaker, Blogger, Minister at Sword and Spirit Ministries International, The Kingdom of Eswatini

"The outstanding book Living Loved by Nqo Mafukidze invites humanity to a place of knowing that Love wants to dwell in us even when we face crisis, betrayal, lack, despair, attacks and even shame. The book removes the reader's veil to discover that you do not need to perform, love is devoted to you no matter what you have or have not done. Nqo Mafukidze takes the reader on a voyage into how Love does not change and allows us to comprehend that when the Father looks at us, all He sees is "good." The must-read Activation after each chapter brings tangible experience to her words and you feel God's presence as you verbalise her words. This is not just a book; it triggers an encounter with Love as a person."

OMACHILE O. ADEYANJU MSc
Co-Founder of Women of Redding, CA, USA
Co-Creator of iBenjamen Studio

"Living Loved is an amazing revelation of who God is, wants and needs to be in our lives if we are to stand firm, immovable, abounding in the work of the Lord; if we are to occupy till Jesus comes and if we are to continue to be about our Father's business till we sleep into an eternity in His Presence, if He tarries. Being a woman who has experienced a lot of pain in my Christian journey, I have learnt that God is still love before, during and after the tragic events. He changeth not. He remains good. He remains God. He remains Love. Praise God for Living Loved because it's filling a gap in Christendom. As you read this book, may this revelation transform you. May you know His loving kindness that is better than life and His mercies that are new every morning."

COMMISSIONER APOSTLE PETUNIA CHIRISERI
Co-Founder of His Presence Ministries International Church, Commissioner of the Zimbabwe Human Rights Commission

"In the most connected but loneliest generation yet, Nqo has touched on a subject that'll heal the world. Starting with the very bride that's been called to love the world, just as God did: the truth is it's experiencing God's love that compels us to love better and henceforth live better! Each page of this book raises the quality of life of the reader just as it raises awareness of the beautiful truth: we were made to live loved."

PHEIM GUTI
Resident Pastor of Forward in Faith Church, Phoenix, Arizona, USA

"Nqo Mafukidze has written a must-read primer for anyone needing a revelation of the nature of God as love. She shares her personal journey i.e. from her fear of God, having low self-esteem to getting the revelation of how much God loves her and ultimately encountering God as love. I encourage you to read this book if you want to experience God's unconditional love. "It is time to live loved!"

PASTOR PRISCILLA WAZARA
Visionary and Pastor of Threshing Floor Prayer Ministries and Birthing a Nation, Pastor of Faith Ministries BCC, Zimbabwe

"We live in a day where love has become god and God sadly isn't experienced as love. There's nothing more important in this life than what Nqo Mafukidze shares about in this book. It's powerfully foundational. If you're triggered by the statement "God is love", if it's offensive or has become a familiar phrase, this book is for you. With an open mind and heart, enjoy being reintroduced to: God is love."

RACHEL DEUSCHLE
Founder - Of Nomad Collective Jewellery Brand
Pastor at Celebration Churches International

"In this book Nqo so eloquently uncovers a great mystery for us. We are taken on a journey that will help one to live in the perpetual experience of the love of God. You'll be activated and challenged to go deeper in your walk with the Lord. She also writes for those who are new to the faith too, so nobody is left behind. My prayer is for you to feel as I do after reading this: living in love and freedom."

RACHEL-YVONNE MCINTOSH
Executive Pastor at Abundant Grace Church, Houston, TX, USA,
Biblical Femininity Coach

"People often ask, "What is love really?" and in Living Loved, Nqo does a splendid job of answering this question. Love "sees you, He knows you and He loves you fully, through and through." Knowing love is knowing God and being loved by Him. This book is a reminder for those who might have forgotten the true nature of the One who is love and an invitation for those who have never known this One. In a refreshing way, Nqo shares parts of her journey to living loved, and through scripture and guided activations, leads readers on their own journeys to denounce lies concerning Love, embrace truth and understand that "living loved is our portion." A worthwhile read."

SHELTER MUSAVENGANA
Author, Writing Consultant and Minister

"The word of God tells us all things work together for good to them that love the Lord. I've always wanted to know what that scripture meant and I found my answer. The book LIVING LOVED explains it all. Regardless of the things that you are going through, God has a purpose and a plan for you. It's coming to the realization that you did not choose God but God chose you. That thing you went through could have killed you, it could have left you in shambles but because God loves you and because he chose you he delivers you from that pain. Even when it doesn't feel like that, know that you are loved. This is a book you need to have even during your Bible study, it leads you to search the scriptures and discover all the dimensions of love. This book is perfect for those who are feeling loved and want to be even deeper in that love, those who are just discovering God's love and also those who once knew God but now feel so unloved."

REBECCA KUCHERERA AKA BECKY K
BBC TV Presenter, ZIFM Radio Host, Confidence Coach Speaker, Voice Over Artist, Moderator, Brand Ambassador

"In an orphan planet, we are born empty, void, desperately grasping for meaning, significance, self-worth and security. Our attempts to meet these needs in one another have caused more harm than good. Love has been used, abused and misused. Unfortunately, Christians are not exempted from the pain, confusion that comes from desperately trying to find, be and give Love. Nqo reintroduces us to not just a feeling but to a person, God is LOVE. She clearly, persuasively and courageously challenges the beliefs, lies, thoughts and preconceived ideas of what Love is and Who Love is. This book is an invitation to not only come face to face with the One who has loved us but to experience HIS unfailing, unending, unadulterated, unquenchable and unequivocal Love as a lifestyle."

BISHOP TENDAYI-DENFORD & PASTOR TSATSA MUTUNGAMIRI
Pastors of Oasis Family Church Harare, Zimbabwe

"In this beautiful book, Nqo doesn't just share thoughts about love, she creates a journey for us to untangle the parts of ourselves that have disconnected from Love and to reconnect with God...Love Himself. It is not only refreshing, but empowering, as she invites us into new mindsets, and it almost feels like she kindly holds our hand as she walks us into more wholeness, more honesty, more love."

TINASHA LARAYE

Leader at Studio Church, Greenville, South Carolina, USA
Poet, Actress, Filmmaker, Speaker, Life Coach, Revolutionary
Founder of MVMNT Collaborative, Miss Black Oklahoma 2007

To us — the men and women who are being reintroduced to God, to Love. As we dare to open our hearts and let Love into the deepest and hidden places of our souls, may we tangibly experience the nature of God as Love. May His presence engulf us. It is time to live like that extravagant, unbridled Love is real and is just for us; because He is.

It's time to live loved!

CONTENTS

Introduction

As a Pastor's kid, I grew up in a Christian and ministry household. From the age of 12, I was serving in church, leading about 300+ people in worship week in week out. Church planting, pastoring people through things, leading a university ministry, leading mission trips, ministry school, travelling nation to nation preaching, you name it, I have been part of it. I am a full on 'church girl'. Don't get me wrong, I am really grateful for my upbringing, my rich heritage in and history with the Lord. I am grateful for my parents' faithfulness to God. This gospel they handed me lit this little girl's soul on fire so much so I have never stopped pursuing and burning for Jesus. I am humbled by all He has done through my surrendered life. There's nothing like experiencing the raw power of God, healing through your own hands, and blind eyes opened right in front of you. It's the stuff of dreams, it's the stuff of the Bible and you can't deny God is real after seeing and being part of that.

Yet in all of that activity and passion to serve God, following His call on my life, He began to show me something wasn't quite right. I was mistaken about an attribute of His nature that is the essence of who He is and it hurt His heart. He didn't just want my works, my Christian activity, or my spiritual gymnastics. The sobering truth was He wanted me. That's all. He is not in this for what we can do for Him. He is not in this for what you can achieve for Him. He is in this for you. *God is Love* and Love wants you. Everything else is a by-product.

Maybe you might identify with parts of my journey. Love wanted me. He had always wanted me but somehow the accuser had crept into my relationship with God who is Love from early on and crippled me with fear of God. Not the healthy, holy, awe inspiring kind of fear of God but the kind of fear that 1 John 4:18 AMP talks about when it says, *"because fear involves [the expectation of divine] punishment, so the one who is afraid [of God's judgement] is not perfected in love [has not grown into a sufficient understanding of God's love]."*

The NKJV says *"fear involves torment"*, oof, that one cuts deep. I lived under this kind of fear. Tormenting fear. I subconsciously believed God was an angry God. In my mind He was skeptical, watching my every move ready to punish and tell me off at the first mistake or stumble.

Oh The Distance

Now, I wouldn't have said it but subconsciously I believed He was distant, far away, cold, yet ever watching, wagging his finger at me, rolling His eyes, forever disappointed in and disapproving of me. It wasn't my whole view of Him but somewhere deep inside that's how I saw Him and therefore how I interacted with Him. It coloured everything else. It was my filter. I could never be good enough for Him and I was a mistake-maker. It not only impacted how I interacted with Him but how I felt about myself, and how I interacted with others. My lens was fear. I lived to not make mistakes, I lived to please people, to not be a disappointment, yet underneath all the works and striving to be good enough, I still believed I was a mistake-maker and maybe even a mistake myself.

However, God in His kindness began to break through all those lies I had believed and show me His true nature, that He is love. He is warm, joyful, available, extravagant, forgiving, understanding, powerful, able, constant, dependable, faithful, trustworthy Love. He is intimate Love, He is safe and He is good. The beginning of 1 John 4:16 AMP says, *"There is no fear in love [dread does not exist]. But perfect (complete, full-grown) love drives out fear."*

He showed me there was a better way to live than in fear. It is His way, the way of Love. And boy will He drive out fear! You see He is agape Love. Agape Love is a pure, intentional, sacrificial love that intentionally and deliberately desires another's greatest good. He is Love that is pure, there is no mixture, no distortion in Him. He sees you, He knows you and He loves you fully, through and through. This love is willful. It's on purpose, not by accident nor by obligation.

Love loves you intentionally. He does not want you to live in dread — that's the enemy. God who is Love desires the greatest good for you. That is His heart towards you. Everything else is a lie of the enemy. The truth is God is Love and His heart, His intentions towards His creation are good. His intentions towards you are good. There is no fear in love.

Come out of Hiding

To my memory, the journey to living loved consciously began about 10 years ago when I was on a working holiday in Hong Kong. I was just a university student back then and the opportunity to be in Hong Kong for the summer was a dream. I mean who wouldn't want to escape the largely cold or damp British summer? While I was in Hong Kong, I had been reading a book that spoke of Woman being the Crown of Creation, the Crescendo of God's creation, and how we don't have to hide.

As I was walking through the humid streets of East Tsim Sha Tsui, sticky and sweaty, rushing to the MTR (their version of the Tube or Subway) I had an encounter with Love. Suddenly Holy

Spirit asked me, "Do you realise that you walk with your head down, avoiding eye contact and hiding?" It was simple, quiet, just a voice or thought in my head that felt a bit different, it wasn't me and it was kind in its tone. It was Love. Honestly I could've ignored and missed it. It was subtle and yet it was an invitation to a conversation with Love that has lasted years. It was jarring because Love was asking me an uncomfortable question. All my messy bits, my hurt bits, my negative lens of who He was and who I was were tucked away, neatly hidden, swept under the carpet and I was comfortable with it. I honestly didn't realise it until that question. Yet here was Love knocking at the door of my heart, extending an invitation to sift through my heart things and get to really know Him.

"Do you realise that you walk with your head down, avoiding eye contact and hiding?" Bam! It hit me like a ton of bricks. The web of lies that had caused me to live ashamed of just being, was brought into the light. I thought God had a negative filter when looking at me and so I saw and carried myself as such. Those negative feelings I had of how God saw me were even manifesting in how I walked and behaved, down to avoiding eye contact!

It had knocked my confidence in simply being. But Holy Spirit was about to take me on a journey of undoing all of that and teaching me to not only know in my head but also in my heart just how loved I am by God. That He really is Love and absolutely, totally and completely adores me.

In turn I would grow to genuinely love myself too. And I am still growing because it is a lifelong adventure! We can never exhaust who Love is and what that means for us and the world around us.

Encountering Love and learning to love myself led me to helping others encounter Him too. It is my joy to introduce people to Jesus, to Love personified. This is the invitation He has for you today. An invitation to really know Him.

He is the God, Love who holds you, embraces you, rescues you, saves you, delivers you and is your ever present help in time of need. He is for you and not against you. It is His joy to be your God and Father. Yes, in the highs and lows of life, He is a good Father and He is Love.

You are not an orphan, you are loved and you belong. *You can live loved.* You are "the joy set before Him" for which Jesus endured the cross, died and rose again victorious. It was all for a relationship with you, that you would deeply and intimately know Him. You are His greatest treasure. Love wants you.

Living Loved ACTIVATION GUIDE

As we journey together into Living Loved, we will be doing an Activation at the end of each chapter throughout the book. This activation is important because the Bible says, *"For as he thinks in his heart, so is he."* (Proverbs 23:7 NKJV).

This shows that our thoughts determine the outcome of our lives — we become our thoughts. The thoughts that live in our minds shape us. Notice I said the thoughts that *live* not the thoughts that go through. There is a difference between thoughts that live in our minds and the thoughts that simply go through our minds. The thoughts that we allow to park and live in our minds begin to inform and shape our mindset and belief system which in turn impacts our actions and our reality. The thoughts that go through our minds cannot shape us, we don't give them a chance to.

If our (live in) thoughts are not aligned with God's thoughts about us, we are going to live beneath what God has for us. We will be like the older son in the story often called the story of the prodigal son, Luke 15:11-32. He was mad at his father for throwing his younger brother who had sinned and disgraced the family a party yet he (the older son) had always done what was expected of him. His father said to him, *"Son, you are always with me, and all that I have is yours."* (v.31) This is an eye opener.

The older son had been living in his father's house but not accessing everything that was available to him! He had limited thinking and it shaped his life. He became bitter, angry and jealous, feeling victimized and deprived yet all along it was all his! He had full access to all his father had. He just didn't realise what was his as a son.

When we don't understand our identity and place as children of God, we shut ourselves out from all He has made available to us in His love. Living loved is our portion, yet we may become frustrated and feel deprived simply because our thinking is not in alignment with what God says about us. Our mindset can limit us from experiencing Love; from experiencing just how good God is. This is why we must break agreement with the lies of the enemy and align our thoughts with Love's thoughts. Confessions are a powerful way to do this.

We may have come into agreement with these lies knowingly or unknowingly. There is no condemnation whatsoever in this. Life happens to all of us. The enemy comes for all of us. As life happens and we have negative experiences, negative thoughts contrary to God's word can pop up. It's easy to accept these lies as truth when we are unaware, tired, overwhelmed, hurt, and the lies feel so real. That's when they become our belief system and shape our lives. The good news is Jesus says we are not orphans! We have not been left alone and abandoned. He is Love and He will come to us. (John 14:18) We are not alone in this. We are not weak and we are not powerless. God's word shows us that there is creative power in our tongues and words.

This Activation is the part where we directly address what we believe. Where we take back our power from the enemy. Where we receive or activate the sound mind God gave us. As you get to the end of each chapter, intentionally become aware of Holy Spirit with you in that moment. Take a deep breath, quieten your heart and mind. Be open to experiencing God as Love as you break agreement with lies and agree with truth. Posture your heart to hear from and receive Love. It might be simple and soft, it might be loud, but He is with you. You are a child of God. You have authority and power through Jesus to tear the lies down and see truth established in your mind, heart, spirit and body. You are going to use that power to break ties with the enemy's lies that have held you captive. You will then come into agreement with, receive and activate the truth of God's word in your life, empowering you to live loved.

Here are some scriptures that will help you understand the impact of this Activation:

"A man will be satisfied with good by the fruit of his mouth"
– Proverbs 12:14 NKJV

"Death and life are in the power of the tongue, and those who love it and indulge it will eat its fruit and bear the consequences of their words."
– Proverbs 18:21 AMP

"For God has not given us a spirit of fear, but of power and of love and of a sound mind."
– 2 Timothy 1:7 NKJV

"For God did not give us a spirit of timidity or cowardice or fear, but [He has given us a spirit] of power and of love and of sound judgment and personal discipline [abilities that result in a calm, well-balanced mind and self-control]."
– 2 Timothy 1: 7 AMP

"For though we walk in the flesh, we do not war according to the flesh. For the weapons of our warfare are not carnal but mighty in God for pulling down strongholds, casting down arguments and every high thing that exalts itself against the knowledge of God, bringing every thought into captivity to the obedience of Christ"

– 2 Corinthians 10:3-5 NKJV

I invite you to choose life and bring those thoughts into the obedience of Christ each time you do the Activation. It's time for freedom. God is Love and He is for you. You get to live loved.

When you reach the Activation at the end of each chapter, you will find a section with lies to break agreement with and truths you can come into agreement with relating to each chapter. This is not to limit you to those ones only but to kick off your conversation with Love Himself and your freedom journey. Allow Holy Spirit to reveal more, He wants to minister to you and it is beautiful.

Here is an example of what this section will look like:
Say this out loud or within yourself...

BREAKING AGREEMENT WITH LIES:

I break agreement with the lie that God is not Love.
I break agreement with the lie that I have to hide.
I break agreement with the lie that I am a mistake.

AGREEING WITH TRUTH:

I come into agreement with the truth that God is Love and Love is for me.

I come into agreement with the truth that I can fully be, no hiding.
I come into agreement with the truth that I am not a mistake, I was made intentionally by God.

When you get to these sections, feel free to say the words in the Activation out loud or whisper if you are in a place to. If you are not in a place to say this out loud then simply say it in your heart and mind. Be assured by the scriptures below that God hears you and He will every single time.

"I'm an open book to you; even from a distance, you know what I'm thinking."
– Psalm 139:2 MSG

"For there is not a word on my tongue, but behold, O Lord, You know it altogether."
– Psalm 139:4 NKJV

If you identified any other lies, limited/limiting beliefs through thoughts and feelings coming up as you read this, that may be Holy Spirit highlighting them or them kicking against truth coming into your heart. Do the exercise above with them too. If you are in a place to, then verbally break agreement with the lies and agree with the opposite, God's word and truth. Feel free to do this at any point as you read each chapter and throughout your days as thoughts and feelings come up. Ask Holy Spirit to help you identify lies and show you what the truth is. It's absolutely ok if you need to repeat the phrases over and over silently or out loud until the truth sinks in from your head to your heart. This can take time and thankfully God has all the time in the world for you. Your heart, mind, will and emotions are a priority. Your soul is a priority to God. He cares about your soul doing well. *"Beloved, I pray that you may prosper in all things and be in health, just as your soul prospers."* (3 John 1:2 NKJV).

Finally, take time to listen for Love's thoughts and voice throughout your day. He could say anything! Jesus said His sheep hear His voice in John 10:27, so expect Him to speak to you. David said His thoughts for us are more in number than the sand on the seashore (Psalm 139:17-18). He wants to speak to you. It could be as simple as a passing thought, a feeling or desire, a picture that flashes through your mind or vision, something someone says to you or something that pops up through your day and even dreams when you go to sleep.

If you are not sure, the way you know it's Him is that His words communicate His love for you, encourage you or lovingly call you to be the best version of yourself, to be everything He made you to be. He is much kinder than we think Him and more often than we are to ourselves even in His correction.

I've provided some space to write down what He says to you throughout your days at the end of each chapter. I encourage you to write or record what He says to you wherever you feel comfortable. It's always so precious to look back on our encounters with Love and experience Him in that way all over again and more. It's your history with Him and it carries value.

I'm so excited for you and the wonderful things Love is about to do in your life! So my friend, let the adventure into Living Loved begin.

— chapter one —

Let's Be Real.

"God is Love"
– 1 John 4:16 AMP

"God *is* love". Let's be real, in the culmination of trying to juggle making a living, family, friendships, relationships, sifting through or just coping in spite of deeply buried childhood traumas, making life decisions, and desiring more for our lives; it can all be overwhelming. Encountering Love in the midst of it all can feel so far-fetched. We find ourselves dealing with individual and collective trauma, loss, grief, global crises and grappling with sin. Then there's the rollercoaster of emotions that come with hope, faith, and oh disappointment, when things don't work out the way we expected and life is just...well, life-ing.

In all that, the statement "God is love" can feel offensive, idealistic and contrary to reality and what is possible as our daily experience. We may think, "it's impossible", "it's too good to be true", "it's for someone else, definitely not me." Oh but it is for you, He is for you!

Love knows how to wade through all of that and meet your heart. He desires to meet you right where you are. In reality it's what He does. He is a humble Love. Think about it. King of Kings, Lord of Lords, leaves heaven's throne just to come for us, to die for us, before we even knew of or loved Him. Meeting us right where we were at, and still comes for us today; He avails Himself to us. He wants to meet us right where we are. Isn't that Love?

"God is love". It's a phrase we hear often in Christendom. It's scripture and it's said frequently enough that we may have become familiar with it, too familiar in fact. We've heard it so much, we process it as basic knowledge in our minds, an elementary lesson. There is a danger when we hear something a lot to think we know it and so skip over, rush through and not pay attention the next time we come across it. We don't savour it. We feel like it's a class we already took and passed, yet it may only be head knowledge.

Sadly, many of us may not experience this God who is Love as deeply or as often as He created us to. His desire is for us to abide, to live in His love. To not just have head knowledge, but experiential knowledge of His nature as Love. There is an invitation to more. Since He is Love and He lives in us, our entire life's existence should be a Love encounter! It can be. We can walk with Love in a practical way.

1 John 4:16 AMP says, *"We have come to know [by personal observation and experience], and have believed [with deep,* consistent *faith] the love which God has for us. God is love, and the one who abides in love abides in God, and God abides* continually *in him."*

Whoa, this sounds like we can actually *live loved.* Even in the midst of life doing its thing, trying to make good decisions and sometimes failing to do so and the enemy attacking us, *we can* intimately and powerfully experience this God, Love and live like that Love is real and is for us. Because He is. We can abide, we can *live* in this Love. There is an invitation here. In the midst of the chaos, Love is offering a safe place, encounter, experiential knowledge of His nature, an invitation to not only visit Love here and there but to abide, dwell, live in Love Himself consciously.

He is more powerful than the chaos and He can hold you in the midst of it. Love will cut through the noise if we allow Him to. The key is in opening our hearts to Him. It's in choosing to let Him protect us instead of self-protecting and inevitably shutting Him out with everything else.

But How Though?

You may be wondering how one can encounter this God, Love and live in His reality? How can you *live loved*?

In Matthew 22:36-39 NKJV a lawyer asked Jesus this question, *"Teacher, which is the great commandment in the law?"* Jesus said to him, *"You shall love the Lord your God with all your heart, with all your soul, and with all your mind." This is the first and great commandment. And the second is like it: 'You shall love your neighbour as yourself.'"*

And then 1 John 4:19 NKJV gives us the key to the first part of the great commandment, *"We love Him because He first loved us."* We can only love Him because He first loved us. All the outworking and outflow of love through our lives is meant to come from one place: encountering His love. He first loved us! That's where we start. He is the source. He shows us how. We can't do the rest in a healthy or sustainable way unless we first sit with Him, sit with Love and let Love love us. *Encountering God's love is the key to living loved.* When we encounter how He loved us first, we can't help but to love Him with our whole being, love ourselves well and then love our neighbour as ourselves.

Let's be real. Along my journey of opening up my heart to encounter the nature of God as Love, I have found that it is incredibly vulnerable. Feeling vulnerable, naked, our inner world seen as it is, can be scary. This journey can involve lots of tears as we break up with and let go of the lies of the enemy and dare to believe God's truth about who He is, what He is like and who we are to Him. Yet when we accept the invitation to this adventure, soon enough we begin to believe Him. The lies fall off as we begin to believe He is Love, experience His love and choose to *live loved.*

No One is Disqualified

God is Love. I have seen grown men and women weep as they have encountered Love. No one is exempt. No one is disqualified. You are not too young, you are not too old, you are not too serious, you are not too sinful, you are not too ugly; you are not too anything! Neither are you not (fill in the blank) enough! You're just right. You're just the person Jesus came for. Love is for you. *"For God so loved the world (that's you and me) that He gave His only begotten Son..." (John 3:16 NKJV).* Love came with you in mind. Jesus came with love as His motive. It was all love.

This book will take you on an adventure to encounter Love. I encourage you to open your heart. Take time to savour the words. Let Love be real with you. Be real with Love. Let Love's truth seep into your heart. Let God's truth change you from the inside out. Do not skim over the familiar phrases, the familiar scriptures. Read every word as if this is the first time you have ever come across it. Give it your full attention. Choose to be fully present and experience every sentence like it's alive. The breath of God is on this book and He will awaken you to His Love nature. As offensive as this Love may be to fears long held, rejection long settled into, skepticism long devoted to or life shaping disappointments, this is your invitation to a new place. A real place. To the way of living you were created for. The way of Love. Living Loved. This is your invitation to freedom.

Here's my prayer for you. You can join me in it too: With each page, each word, I invite you Holy Spirit to reveal God who is Love to your precious child reading this. I echo the prayer of Paul in Ephesians 3:17-19 AMPC, *"May Christ through your faith [actually] dwell (settle down, abide, make His permanent home) in your hearts! May you be rooted deep in love and founded securely on love, that you may have the power and be strong to apprehend and grasp with all the saints [God's devoted people, the experience of that love] what is the breadth and length and height and depth [of it]; [That you may really come] to know [practically, through experience for yourselves] the love of Christ, which far surpasses mere knowledge [without experience]; that you may be filled [through all your being] unto all the fullness of God [may have the richest measure of the divine Presence, and become a body wholly filled and flooded with God Himself]!" Amen.*

Now then my friend, it's time to Lived Loved!

Living Loved.

ACTIVATION

(If you need a refresher on any part of the Activation at any point, feel free to pop back to the Activation Guide)

Say this out loud or within yourself...

BREAKING AGREEMENT WITH LIES:

I break agreement with the lie that I cannot hear God's voice.
I break agreement with the lie that I cannot experience God's Love.
I break agreement with the lie that it's too late for me to encounter Love deeply.

AGREEING WITH TRUTH:

I come into agreement with the truth that I hear God's voice.
I come into agreement with the truth that I have the capacity to experience God as Love.
I come into agreement with the truth that Love wants me and it's never too late. There is more for me.

I receive You Love and I choose to Live Loved. God, I give You permission to take me on this journey of encountering You as Love and living loved.

LOVE'S THOUGHTS TO ME TODAY:

— chapter two —

Love Can Handle You.

"Love is patient,..."
– 1 Corinthians 13:4 NIV

"Love suffers long..."
– NKJV

"Love never gives up..."
– MSG

"Love is large and incredibly patient..."
– TPT

"Love endures with patience and serenity..."
– AMP

Since God is Love, this means God is patient. He is large and *incredibly* patient. God suffers long, endures with patience and serenity. He never gives up on you. And this Love is not just for your neighbour, that highly intelligent and capable colleague or that friend or family member you feel is more deserving or worthy of this kind of Love. This God, this Love *is* for you.

The God who created the heavens and the earth says you are worthy of that kind of Love. You are worth His patience. It's not based on what you do or do not do. You cannot earn this Love. Neither can you lose this Love. He made you and so He loves you. He made you and so He is patient with you. He made you and so you are worthy of Love, of God. He decided so and so it is. It's not because of anything you have done but because of who He is. He made you as an object of His love and affection. He made you to be with Him.

It's wild and offensive to our human minds but this is Love. This is God. He says you are worthy, worth it, you have worth. He loves you because He loves you, because He loves you, because He loves you, because He *is* Love. Love can handle you. He made you to be loved. You were made already loved by Him.

God, Love loved you first. Love saw you first. Love chose you first. Before you were born, He loved you. Before you ever did anything, He loved you. Before you knew Him, He loved you. Before you lived for Him, He loved you. *"We love Him because He first loved us."* (1 John 4:19 NKJV). You had His full attention before you ever lifted a finger. You had His full affection before you ever did a thing. Nothing you do could ever stop God loving you. Nothing you do could ever cut you off from His patience. Love can handle you.

Life can be busy, good, complicated, draining all at once, in sections or in phases! People we love and who love us can be busy, have other priorities before us and sometimes or (often!) become impatient with us. It's just life and that's ok. We are all growing. As human beings we have limited physical and emotional capacity and that means we are not large enough to handle everyone in our lives all the time, giving them our full attention.

Stop Scrapping

The thing is sometimes we can project our human limitations on God and therefore on His nature and capacity to be Love to us. We can feel like we are too much, over the top, too messy, we take up too much space, too much time, and are too needy. Yet the first thing 1 Corinthians 13, "The Love chapter" as it's sometimes called, tells us about what Love is like is that He is — large and *incredibly* patient. He suffers *long*. Not short. Not just a little patient, not just a smidge, He's not a small limited Love, He doesn't have a short fuse with you that could blow anytime. His capacity is not small. He's not running out. You're not scrapping the barrel for Love. God is large and incredibly patient with you. He can handle you. He is large enough. He is big enough. There is enough of Him to go around. He can endure whatever is thrown at Him. You can never overwhelm Him, you can never exhaust Him, finish Him, get Him at the end of His rope. No, no, no! He has more than enough room, time, space, forgiveness, patience; He is more than enough Love and *all* that Love is directed at you. Love can handle you.

King David described his experience of the nature of God as Love beautifully in many of the Psalms. Here are a couple of verses from one of my favourite Love Psalms: *"How precious also are Your thoughts to me, O God! How great is the sum of them! If I should count them, they would be more in number than the sand; when I awake, I am still with You."* (Psalms 139:17-18 NKJV).

David had this revelation of Love as One that fiercely pursued, joyfully doted on and protectively surrounded Him. This whole chapter describes how known and valued by God he felt. He experientially knew this large and incredibly patient Love that endures. He experienced the preciousness of Love's thoughts towards him. He was in awe and aware of how innumerable they were!

The Father's Chuckle

One day I became aware of this feeling and fear within me that I could exhaust God's Love. I felt the Father chuckle at me, at the fact that somehow I thought that I could finish His Love, that He could get fed up with me and be done, that it could be too much for Him; that I could be too much for Him. As I wrestled with this limited thinking and feeling, God said to me, "There is no way your husband could love you more than I do". That's when my eyes became teary.

You see, my husband Dylan is the kindest soul I have ever met. He is gentle, loving, understanding, forgiving. I am far from perfect and yet he gives me so many chances to do better, he lovingly challenges me to be the best version of myself, he forgives readily and he is just so patient. He truly believes in me and intentionally makes room for me to be. And that's an amazing but limited human being! God's point in using him as an example was to drive into my heart the truth that no human (no matter how incredible) can ever out-give Him!

Think of the most loving person in your life or that you have ever met. God says "I am infinitely larger and more patient with you than that love and I am for you. I understand you, from the little things to the big things. I have all the room, patience, space and time in the world for you. You are the object of My Love and affection. Take your time. We can do this together."

My friend, living loved is what you were made for. Love can handle you. He is patient enough.

ACTIVATION

Say this out loud or within yourself...

BREAKING AGREEMENT WITH LIES:

I break the lie that I am too much.
I break the lie that I have to earn Your love.
I break agreement with the lie that I could ever exhaust Your love for me God.

AGREEING WITH TRUTH:

I come into agreement with the truth that You created me to be loved by You.
I come into agreement with the truth that You will never ever run out of Love for me.
I come into agreement with the truth that You, God who is Love, are large and incredibly patient with me (insert your name).

LOVE'S THOUGHTS TO ME TODAY:

— *chapter three* —

A Thoughtful Love.

"love... is kind;..."
– 1 Corinthians 13:4 NKJV

"...love is kind and thoughtful..."
– AMP

"...Love cares more for others than for self..."
– MSG

"...Love is gentle and consistently kind to all..."
– TPT

This means God is kind and thoughtful. He is gentle. Sometimes we have this subconscious belief that God is cruel or malicious; that this Love is too good to be true and there's got to be a catch. But those are just lies of the enemy to keep us bound by fear and living beneath the vastness and freedom of Love God created us to live in.

This belief that God is cruel and even hateful may come from a variety of things. It could be through experiencing hard things in life, pain and difficulty, a high performance and perfectionist environment, a highly critical culture or upbringing, being hurt by people we love or those who were meant to protect us but failed, and more. It could also come from a misunderstanding of the Old Testament and how we see God interact with humanity in it.

God is the same yesterday, today and forever. You see, the Old Testament revealed humanity's need for a saviour after the fall, our inability to meet the righteous and just requirement of the Law which was fulfilled by Jesus on our behalf on the cross. Jesus is the express image of God, (Hebrews 1:3 NKJV), when we see Him (in all His kindness and love), we see the Father (John 14:9 NKJV). He is perfect theology. But when we misunderstand humanity's history with God through the Old to the New testament, when we misunderstand His-story and journey with us to redemption, we can see God in a negative light. There is mystery in the gospel and our relationship with God, there are things we won't ever understand on this side of eternity and yet it does not change His nature. He is love and He is for us.

With all those various reasons why we may believe God to be cruel etc., self-protection says to watch out because it could happen again, the pain, hurt, disappointment. Shut your heart down, don't let love in because love hurts. Life is not kind, keep your walls up. I understand this all too well.

The thing is, living like that robs us of the joy, the healing, the comfort, the peace, the adventure that comes with letting Love in in all of His kindness and thoughtfulness. It robs us of experiencing just how loved we are. It's hard to experience His goodness when we shut Him out. We rob ourselves of a full life when we allow our view of God's nature, Love's nature to be shaped by the actions of broken people, circumstances or the enemy's doing.

One-day God said to me, "All I have for you is Love." And He marked my heart with this scripture: ""*Israel, out looking for a place to rest, met God out looking for them!*" God told them,

"I've never quit loving you and never will. Expect love, love, and more love!" (Jeremiah 31:2-6 MSG). You're the one He has on His heart and mind. He is looking out for you.

God *is* kind and thoughtful. He is everlasting Love. When you expect harshness, here comes kindness, when you feel you deserve to be isolated and forgotten, here He comes with His thoughtfulness. When you think your desires are insignificant, He wants to show you what matters to your heart matters to Him. All He has for you is Love.

When we have run so hard for God, given everything, are at the end of ourselves, seeing no progress, depressed and maybe even feeling like it would be better if we were not alive, it's really hard to see and believe the goodness and kindness of God. I know what that feels like. It's hard to believe He is thoughtful there.

We find Elijah was in such a state in 1 Kings 19. Yet God in His kindness and thoughtfulness sent an angel to give him food and he slept. God was intentional to refresh him and give him strength for the journey ahead. He experienced the kindness and thoughtfulness of God in the midst of darkness and depression. God's nature as Love met him there.

You may have had a really hard journey. You may be feeling hurt, burnt out and at the end of your rope. I am sorry that you are in that place. God feels your heart, He catches your tears (Psalms 56:8) and He cares. You are not an afterthought. I want you to know He is sending help. There is refreshing and strength for you here in His kindness and thoughtfulness. He is coming for you in His compassion. You are not alone. He has not abandoned you. He is meeting you here.

Living Loved.

"He's gone into your future to prepare the way, and in kindness He follows behind you to spare you from the harm of your past. He has laid His hand on you!"
– Psalms 139:5 TPT

Living Loved is your destiny.

ACTIVATION

Say this out loud or within yourself...

BREAKING AGREEMENT WITH LIES:

I break agreement with hopelessness.
I break agreement with depression, anxiety and suicide.
I break agreement with the lie that God is cruel, malicious and unkind.

AGREEING WITH TRUTH:

I come into agreement with the truth that God is kind and thoughtful to me (insert name).
I come into agreement with the truth that I matter, I am worth God's kindness and thoughtfulness.
I come into agreement with the truth that I am loved and loveable. I belong and I will live a full life in God.
I receive You Love and I choose to Live Loved.

LOVE'S THOUGHTS TO ME TODAY:

— chapter four —

Goodness!

"...It refuses to be jealous when blessing comes to someone else..."
– 1 Corinthians 13:4 TPT

"...is not jealous or envious;..."
– AMP

"...does not envy;..."
– NKJV

God, who is Love, is not jealous of you. Yeah I said it. This might seem an odd one but I've noticed times in my life where I felt like I've experienced God's goodness but it might just run out. Subconsciously I've realised at times I thought God was holding out on me, like He doesn't want me to have good things. For some reason I treated and saw Him like a stingy Master, as if He would be jealous if I got good. As if He doesn't really want blessings to come to me, like He just wants to keep everything to and for Himself, after all He is the only one deserving!

But God, Love in His kindness, came and tore all those lies apart. He is not jealous of or against us; that is not His nature! He is a generous God, everything He has, He has made available to and for us; that was the point of the cross!

Jesus died so that we might have life and life more *abundantly* (John 10:10). We are not dealing with a jealous taskmaster, we're in an eternal relationship with the Creator of the universe. He made us His children and decided we have access to... well, everything! He is not jealous of us; He is jealous for us. I'll go into that a bit more later.

I want to assure you that all He has for you is good! Goodness, good intentions, a good heart, good outcomes. He is Love.

Right from the beginning, we find the enemy in Genesis 3 convinced us as humanity that God was holding out on us. It's his oldest trick. Adam and Eve were already made in the image and likeness of God (Genesis 1:26-27). They had access to everything in the garden, they were created to rule and reign, to have dominion over all the earth and all that God had made. There was just one tree God said they shouldn't touch or eat, just one. So the sneaky serpent came along saying, *"For God knows that when you eat from it your eyes will be opened, and you will be like God, knowing good and evil."* (Genesis 3:5 NIV).

The issue with that statement is that God had already said they were like Him! We are like Him! That's how He created us in the first place. The devil convinced Eve and in effect Adam that God was holding out on them, withholding good from them, which was a lie!

Not Withholding

Dear one, today I don't know what you are facing but I want to assure you God, Love is not withholding good from you. He is not stingy, He is not jealous, He is generous! He said, *"Let Us make man in Our image, according to Our likeness; let them have dominion... over all the earth"* (Genesis 1:26). His word also says, *"He who did not spare His own Son, but gave Him up for us all, how shall He not with Him also freely give us all things?"* (Romans 8:32).

Love has chosen you and He is never going to change His mind about you. *"In this the love of God was manifested toward us, that God has sent His only begotten Son into the world, that we might live through Him. In this is love, not that we loved God, but that He loved us and sent His Son to be the propitiation for our sins."* (1 John 4:9-10).

God, Love says because of the cross of Jesus and the resurrection, when the Father looks at you, He sees you like He sees Jesus! You are literally the righteousness of God in Christ Jesus (2 Corinthians 5:21). In God's eyes you are just like His Son. In His generosity that's what God has given us as His children. "Love has been perfected among us in this: that we may have *boldness* in the day of judgement; because as He is, so are we in this world." (1 John 4:17).

In Luke 12 Jesus talks about us setting our treasure in heaven and not focusing on earthly things, knowing full well that if He takes care of the lilies, of the birds of the air, of the grass then He will definitely take good care of us! He knows the things we need and we are of much more value to Him than the birds or flowers. As we seek after His Kingdom and His righteousness first, all the other things will be added to us. His heart is good. It is His good pleasure to give us the Kingdom He said. He wants good things for us, He's not stingy, He is not holding back from us. He is jealous for us. He longs for us. He longs for you.

Jealous for You

Now what do I mean when I say He is jealous for you? Throughout the Bible, we find instances where God refers to Himself or is referred to as a jealous God. But this is not the kind of jealousy we've been talking about in this chapter up to now, *"for you shall worship no other god, for the Lord, whose name is Jealous, is a jealous God"* (Exodus 34:14 NKJV).

You see, the kind of jealousy this refers to is like the one of a lover for the love of their life. He is a God who does not want to share us with any other god, any idol, anything that would try to put itself above Him in priority or importance in our lives and hearts, in effect becoming a god to us, somehow controlling our lives or hearts. He longs for us; His heart yearns to have our whole hearts. Fully surrendered to Him as He is fully committed to us. You see He is besotted with you.

All He Sees is Good

I remember being in a season where God was calling me to greater surrender. He was asking me to get out of the boat and walk on the water with Him as it were. It was really scary and what He had promised me on the other side seemed impossible, too good to be true, too big and yet I dared to believe His goodness, give Him my full surrender and go wherever He called me. I had an encounter in that season where I saw a picture. It was like we were on the top of a mountain looking across a landscape. Then He said to fearful little me that He had looked ahead into the future (my future) and *all* He saw was good. Nothing else. Only good.

Today as you let go of the image of a God who is jealous of you, stingy, and holding back from you, I want you to embrace the God who stands in this very moment with you. Whether it's joyous, full of hope, excitement or like I was, you're terrified, in the waiting for seemingly impossible miracles, venturing into unfamiliar territory, can't see how good could possibly come from your situation; He stands here with you. He looks far ahead into your future and all He sees is good because all He has for you is good. Living loved is your portion.

ACTIVATION

Say the following out loud or within yourself...

BREAKING AGREEMENT WITH LIES:

I break the lie that God is stingy and not generous.
I break the lie that God is withholding good from me.
I break the lie that God would ever withhold good from me.

AGREEING WITH TRUTH:

I come into agreement with the truth that God longs for me.
I come into agreement with the truth that God only has good things for me.
I come into agreement with the truth that God is extravagantly generous towards me.

LOVE'S THOUGHTS TO ME TODAY:

— chapter five —

Love Chooses You.

"Love does not brag about one's achievements nor inflate its own importance."
– 1 Corinthians 13:4 TPT

"Love does not brag and is not proud or arrogant."
– AMP

"Love does not parade itself, is not puffed up;"
– NKJV

It is mind-blowing to me that God, the King of Kings, Lord of Lords, Creator of the universe, of all things we know and those we don't, chose me. He chose you. This is His nature, our Servant King. Jesus said the greatest among us is the one who serves (Luke 22:26). He modelled what that servant leadership, empty of pride and arrogance looks like. He showed us what God, Love, is like when He washed the disciples' feet, when He chose to die in our place though He was fully God, completely sinless and faultless. He humbled Himself to the point of death, just for you and me. What a humble Love. He decided somehow our lives were more important than His own. He says you are to die for!

I was singing a worship song to the Lord one day that speaks of His worthiness. It was beautiful and I could feel His presence with me as I poured out my heart to Him in exaltation. It was a holy moment as I sang "You are worthy of it all". Suddenly I heard Him say, "Do not come to me like a nothing. I never made nothings. I made people of dominion to walk in the cool of the garden with Me." That struck me and I was hit by His greatness, His worthiness and vastness all over again. I was hit by the vastness of Love all over again.

He is just so big, so great, so awe inspiring yet He made room for us in Him. We can take up space. The King is not threatened by us, He invites us into His royalty and calls us Kings and Priests to our God (Revelation 1:6). We have a place in and with Him. You have a place in and with Him. You can take up space. This servant King humbled Himself in order to lift us up. He died so we could live. A divine exchange. He took what we deserved because of sin and gave us all that He is. He made us new and clean. What a King. What a Love. What a God. A humble Love.

This God, Love, does not brag, is not puffed up, prideful nor arrogant and distant. He came down to our level. He makes Himself friend, accessible to anyone who comes to Him. He affirms us, makes room for us, dignifies us though we in ourselves are not deserving and could never do enough to earn this. He looks over all the reasons why we are not worthy and or deserving and He says but we are. Made in His image, marked by sin because of the fall, He considered our lives more important than His. He humbled Himself to the point of death on a cross just for us. We didn't deserve a defense, yet looking at us through His eyes of Love, His mercy and grace He became our defense. Sinless and spotless. Love divine, beyond anything this world can offer, He chose us. He chose you. He laid Himself down for you and I. He chooses us now. He chooses you now and forever. He left glory just to have you.

He looked at death and said you are worth it. What a humble Love. What a God!

Our Servant King

This God, this servant King, this Love is not condescending, judging or patronizing. He does not look down on you and belittle you. He is God, exalted on high, glorified, King of all Kings, King of all things, the only true God, yet He chose to come and not only save us, restore us to Himself, make a way for us to be with Him forever as His children but even further He chooses to dwell, to live in us through Holy Spirit.

> *"And I will pray the Father, and He will give you another Helper, that He may abide with you forever— the Spirit of truth, whom the world cannot receive, because it neither sees Him nor knows Him; but you know Him, for He dwells with you and will be in you. I will not leave you orphans; I will come to you."*
>
> ***– John 14:16-18 NKJV***

God is just a Father who wants His children back. Love is just a Father who wants His children close. He refused to leave us orphans, abandoned, with no carers, no parents, alone. He chose to come for us and He comes for you even now. He will never stop coming for you. He wants to live inside you.

Life can harden us and He knows that. Yet there is an invitation in this moment to open up. To allow Him to Daddy you as He often asks me to do. I know some of you may cringe at that phrase but He said it to me. And He has an invitation for you that you will relate with. Would you open your heart to receive Him? To receive this Love that refuses to abandon you? Would you allow yourself to engage with the One who chose you and continues to choose you?

There is nothing like this Love and He is for you. You have a Father. You are not an orphan. You are chosen. You are worth it. Living loved is your birthright.

ACTIVATION

Say the following out loud or within yourself...

BREAKING AGREEMENT WITH LIES:

I break the lie that I am inferior.
I break the lie that I am a nothing.
I break the lie that I am worthless.

AGREEING WITH TRUTH:

I come into agreement with the truth that I have value.
I come into agreement with the truth that I am righteous.
I come into agreement with the truth that I am worth the blood of Jesus.
I come into agreement with the truth that I am a King/Queen and a Priest to God through Jesus.

LOVE'S THOUGHTS TO ME TODAY:

— *chapter six* —

Shame Can Go to Hell!

"...Love does not traffic in shame and disrespect, nor selfishly seek its own honour..."
– 1 Corinthians 13:5

"...It is not rude; it is not self-seeking,..."
– AMP

"...Does not behave rudely..."
– NKJV

Shame is defined as a feeling of embarrassment or humiliation that arises in relation to the perception of having done something dishonourable, immoral, or improper (*verywellmind*). Another definition is a painful feeling of humiliation or distress caused by the consciousness of wrong or foolish behaviour *(Collins Dictionary)*.

Some have also described shame as the voice that says you are your sin and mistakes. But the truth is you are who God says you are, your mistakes and sin are things you have done not who you are. Guilt says I have done something wrong whereas shame says I am my wrong actions.

Rude is defined as offensive or embarrassing. *(Cambridge Dictionary)*

Listen, Love is not out to shame you. That is not how He behaves. That is not His heart towards you, that is not His attitude towards you. He is not waiting for you to mess up so that He can sneer, laugh and point a finger at you. Instead, He's like the parent who will defend their child fiercely to anyone who dares to accuse them of something (even if they did it!). He is compassionate. He is your fierce defender. He can empathise with you. He genuinely understands what it is like to live in a body, walk on earth and go through everything you go through. He defends us, not the wrong we do, yet He is always in our corner wanting the best for us.

"For we do not have a High Priest who is unable to sympathise and understand our weaknesses and temptations, but One who has been tempted [knowing exactly how it feels to be human] in every respect as we are, yet without [committing any] sin."
– Hebrews 4:15 AMP

He's not out to shame you, He understands you. He is Helper and you don't have to walk this walk alone. One of my favourite prayers to pray is "Holy Spirit help". He is called the Helper because He knew we would need help! Do not be ashamed or embarrassed to call out to the Helper for help. He is not ashamed or embarrassed of you.

Love sees you in your worst state and instead of shaming or embarrassing you, He saves, He protects and He justifies you. He comes to your rescue. Love is not out to rudely offend, humiliate and disrespect you like you have no value. It is simply not in His nature. His nature is Love. He doesn't put you down to feel honoured. He lifts you up to where He is. He clears your name. He says you're seated in Christ in heavenly places, that's where you belong (Ephesians 2:6). And He teaches you how. His way.

He Loved You Then, He Loves You Now

In John 8:1-11 we are introduced to a woman who was caught red handed, in adultery. We don't know what happened to the man she was caught with but the religious leaders in this account were fixated on shaming and embarrassing this woman; maybe she was an easy target. They brought her to Jesus intent on not only shaming and embarrassing her in front of everyone but intent on the law at the time being carried out. "Now Moses, in the law, commanded us that such should be stoned." they said. They wanted to test Jesus, to test Love. They wanted to see if He would join in their shaming of this woman, be rude to her, embarrass and condemn her to what they believed to be the right punishment — a stoning. But Jesus threw a curve ball at them.

He refused to participate in shaming her. He refused to humiliate her. Instead of condemning this woman who was clearly in the wrong, He confronted their own humanity, their own sinfulness, their own weakness, He humbled them. *"He who is without sin among you, let him throw a stone at her first."* One by one they walked away. Convicted. They were not worthy to judge her; they had no right. They were human just like her. Prone to mistakes just like her. They had sinned just like her.

Love stood in her corner when she did not deserve it. He was the only one worthy to judge and condemn her yet all He had for her was Love. He was the only sinless one yet He still refused to traffic in shame and disrespect towards her. I can picture His loving eyes and reassuring voice as He said to her,

"Neither do I condemn you; go and sin no more." Love said she was worth saving that day. Love was bigger than her sin.

Instead of shaming you, He is the way out, He is the solution. He is the way, the truth and the life. He is the one who sees your value underneath all the messiness of life. He is the one who sets you free. He loved you when He died on the cross for you, before you were born, before you knew Him, before you chose Him and before you ever did a single thing for Him. He didn't need your performance in order to love you. He didn't need perfection in order to love you. He didn't need you to earn His love in order to die for you; in order to love you. He doesn't need it now. He loved you then, He loves you now.

Righteous

You were never made to live in shame. Shame came in when Adam and Eve sinned against God but it was not His intent for us. Shame tells you that the wrong you did is who you are, it's your identity. But that's simply not true. If you have accepted Jesus as your Lord and Saviour, you are the righteousness of God (2 Corinthians 5:21). That is your identity, righteous. You are in right standing with God.

That doesn't mean you never make mistakes, but it does mean you don't let them define you and your life. They are not your identity. Proverbs 24:16 says a *righteous* man falls seven times but he gets up again! We don't go around intentionally trying to fall or trying to displease and hurt God's heart. But the point of this scripture is that you might fall, and even fall many times but you don't have to stay down. It doesn't have to define you.

God doesn't define you by your falls. That is the glory of the cross. The mind blowing beauty of the blood of Jesus that washes us clean. You can get back up again. The failure, the falling, the mistakes, the imperfections do not make you unrighteous. You still get to get back up again. You get to choose to get back up again. You get to repent and get back on track. Repentance means simply changing your ways, your direction, changing your way of thinking from one way to another. It is leaving what God has prohibited and returning to what He has commanded. You get to change course from going the wrong way to going the right way. Holy Spirit is always there to help you get back up again.

He's the loving Father who when we slip and fall, when we make mistakes, bad decisions, when we outright sin, lovingly comes to pick us up, dust us off and set us back on the right path. He is the loving Father who sees you at your worst and still adores you, His child, through and through. The one we call the prodigal son knows this very well. Some versions will call him the lost son. We find his story in Luke 15:11-24. He couldn't wait for his dad to die, demanded his inheritance early, went and partied and blew through it all to the point where he was eating pig food because he had nothing left! He decided what he had done was too terrible, he couldn't possibly come back to his dad's house and be treated as a son again. He made a plan. Oh don't we all? He would apologise and ask to be treated as one of the servants. At least they ate much better than what he had been reduced to, he thought.

But Love wasn't holding a grudge, counting his sins against him, waiting to punish, scold, shame and embarrass him. Jesus describes the response of the Father in a way that shows us His nature as Love.

"So the young son set off for home. From a long distance away, his father saw him coming, dressed as a beggar, and great compassion swelled up in his heart for his son who was returning home. The father raced out to meet him, swept him up in his arms, hugged him dearly, and kissed him over and over with tender love. "Then the son said, 'Father, I was wrong. I have sinned against you. I could never deserve to be called your son. Just let me be—' "The father interrupted and said, 'Son, you're home now!' "Turning to his servants, the father said, 'Quick, bring me the best robe, my very own robe, and I will place it on his shoulders. Bring the ring, the seal of sonship, and I will put it on his finger. And bring out the best shoes you can find for my son. Let's prepare a great feast and celebrate. For my beloved son was once dead, but now he's alive! Once he was lost, but now he is found!' And everyone celebrated with overflowing joy.'

– Luke 15:20-24 TPT

Home

You see, God is just a Father who wants His children back. He is just a Father who wants His children home. If you've made bad decisions, mistakes, if you've sinned or maybe due to fear of people or perfectionism you just have the perception like I had that you are just a mistake maker and God sees you as never good enough; the truth is God is not counting anything against you. That is not how He sees you. He just wants you back. Your loving Father wants you home in His presence. He has no shame and embarrassment for you. Only Love. A huge welcome home. Forgiveness. A celebration because you are His beloved. It is His kindness that leads us to repentance (Romans 2:4) and oh how kind He is to us. Sometimes the biggest sin we need to repent of is refusing to let Love love us. Rejecting Him. It's thinking we know better than He does and then distancing ourselves from Him when all He has for us is Love. We can't live a righteous life apart from the righteous One. Let Love love you. Living Loved is possible.

Living Loved.

ACTIVATION

Say the following out loud or within yourself...

BREAKING AGREEMENT WITH LIES:

I break the lie that I am a shameful being.
I break the lie that God is ashamed of me.
I break the lie that I have to live in shame because of what I've done.

AGREEING WITH TRUTH:

I come into agreement with the truth that I am free from shame.
I come into agreement with the truth that Jesus understands me.
I come into agreement with the truth that Jesus loved me then and He loves me now.

LOVE'S THOUGHTS TO ME TODAY:

— chapter seven —

Easy Come, Easy Go!

"...it is not provoked [nor overly sensitive and easily angered]; it does not take into account a wrong endured."
– 1 Corinthians 13:5 AMP

"...Doesn't fly off the handle, doesn't keep score of the sins of others..."
– MSG

"...Love is not easily irritated or quick to take offence."
– TPT

"...is not provoked, thinks no evil;"
– NKJV

Unlike many things and experiences in this world, unlike human love, God, Love, is not easy come, easy go. He will stick it through with you. You don't need to live life walking on eggshells as if you could ever irritate and offend Him so much as to scare Him off. Love experiences you fully and is in it for the long haul with you. I mentioned before how I grew up thinking I was an inconvenience to God, an annoyance really. We can be so afraid to be too much that we just make ourselves nothing, invisible, we hide; afraid to offend, to upset, to anger people around us and God. We can make ourselves so small, thinking we are doing a service to the world when all along we are actually robbing it of the glory of God that is on our lives. The truth is that no one can release the glory of God the way that you can. His expression through you is unlike His expression through anyone else, ever. Just the same way He uniquely made your fingerprint, there's no other like it nor has there ever been or ever will be, His expression through your life is just the same. Your relationship with Him is just as unique and the fragrance of Christ through your life is unique and necessary in this world.

However, when we become so afraid to anger, to irritate; so introspective, and aware of our own mistakes, our own sinfulness, our fears, anxieties, humanity, weakness; all it does is grow those things. What we feed grows. What we focus on grows. It's like when you're driving or riding a bike. You tend to go in the direction your eyes are focusing on.

In the area where I live in Devon, England, there is a farm with a large orange elephant which can be seen from a motorway. It's fun and definitely catches the eye. The thing is, if I'm driving and looking at the elephant, no matter how much I try to drive straight I will end up steering off the road towards the direction the big orange elephant is in! It's the same with all the things that try to steal our attention away from God, from His truth, His nature as Love and who we are in light of His nature. If we focus on them, we'll end up going that way and making them our reality instead of the reality God has for us. We cannot afford to smear God as the accuser because that's not who He is. That's not who Love is. He is not an easy come, easy go kind of love. He is constant.

Fear is such a thief of life. Fear of stepping out of line, fear of being irritating, annoying, inconveniencing, offensive, in the way, messy, real, raw, unfiltered, too much and fear of being a failure or failing. And it's true, people can definitely get easily irritated with us and quickly take offence. We all know what it's like to be on both ends. But God is not like us. He is not limited in capacity like we are. Love is not so weak, so fickle, so changing. He is steady, He is steadfast, He's the one we can always count on. He is not fixated on our weaknesses, on our sins, on our past, on our fears, our mistakes and our imperfections. Love will not fly off the handle at you. He is not easily angered.

In chapter one, we talked at length about His incredible patience, how He is large and He can handle you, *all* of you. He is not easily scared off. In fact, He can't be scared off by you at all. I want you to know God is not intimidated by you.

God is not scared of you. He is not scared of your messiness. He is not afraid of you. Your imperfection does not easily anger Him, neither does it put Him off. It is actually faith that pleases Him. Stepping out when it could all go to pot, obeying Him when it doesn't make sense, using your voice when you feel unqualified or disqualified; getting back up when you have fallen and choosing His way.

When you read through the Bible you find out it wasn't the perfect people who had it all together that God used. (I don't know that those existed even then!). It was David who wore his heart on his sleeve, a feeler, a shepherd boy, overlooked by his dad, belittled and bullied by his brothers. Yet God chose him to be King over His people. And yup, he did have some big messes along the way, like committing adultery with Bathsheba and killing her husband (2 Samuel 11-12). And still God calls him a man after His own heart! (1 Sam. 13:14). It was Esther who was an orphan, she felt totally unqualified to save her people, insecure, undesirable and ignored by the King. In her moment of destiny, she even needed her cousin to give her a kick up the butt for her to step into it and not hide away, making herself small. "Yet who knows whether you have come to the kingdom for such a time as this?" (Esther 4:14), he said. And there are so many more examples of God using imperfect people to write history. This could be you if you kick fear out.

You are not an imposter, you're the real deal, a work of art created by God Himself. You are His masterpiece. Intentionally put on the earth to release His glory, to usher in His Kingdom on earth as it is in heaven. You are a heavenly being in a body on assignment on the earth. An ambassador of Christ. You have what it takes. You are forgiven and you are loved. You can have a fresh new start, a clean slate because of Jesus' mercy. Because of Love's mercy.

God is not scared or intimidated by you. The small things and the big things. He is not appalled. He is not about to lose it at you. Love is big enough to handle you. To Love you. To guide you. To lead you. To adventure with you. To try things with you. You can step out and do it even when you're afraid. Whatever that dream, that vision, that calling is, it's an adventure with God and His priority is relationship with you throughout. He is not irritated by your personality, your quirks, your laugh, your way of thinking; He made you!! He was intentional about how He made you. You're His dream come true. He doesn't just love you, He likes you. He enjoys you. He enjoys your company.

What Score?

Love is not keeping a score of your sins, mistakes and imperfections. Mistakes and imperfections? They're not the end of the world. He's like a loving father or mother teaching their child how to ride a bike. When you fall, He's not annoyed, He's not meanly laughing, He's not angry that you're not getting it. He comes alongside you to help you, encourage you, push you outside your comfort zone, confident you will get it and He will be right there with you. Even if you've been at it a while, Love is not easily angered. He is not the accuser of the brethren (Revelation 12:10); that's the devil who constantly wants to make you feel like you are doing something wrong, whispering in your ear that you're not enough, never good enough, you're a fraud. But all those are lies of the enemy!

Never think that condemnation comes from God because God, Love, is not like that. *"There is therefore now no condemnation to those who are in Christ Jesus, who do not walk according to the flesh, but according to the Spirit."* (Romans 8:1). Love is besotted with you. Love adores you. Love is sure about you. God delights in you, enjoys you, rejoices over you; you put a smile on His face. (Zephaniah 3:17, Psalm 18:19, Psalm 147:11.) Yes, your quirks put a smile on His face.

And sin? Your past, your present, even your future sin? Sin hurts us and it hurts God's heart tremendously. Sin is disobeying what God says is best for us and how we should live our lives. The thing is, when you are in love, you live to please your lover, you don't want to hurt them. It's the same in our relationship with God. We get to live to please Him and not hurt His heart. But if we do, He has made provision for this. *"If we confess our sins, He is faithful and just to forgive us our sins and to cleanse us from all unrighteousness."* (1 John 1:9).

Don't be afraid to come to Him if you do sin. It's not anger waiting for you, its forgiveness, it's another chance, it's a fresh start. It's Love waiting for you. He makes you *completely* clean.

He is not keeping score of the sins, rather He forgives and washes them away. The Bible even says He doesn't remember them! The all-knowing God chooses to forget your sins — *"I, I am He who blots out your transgressions for my own sake, and I will not remember your sins."* (Isaiah 43:25). *"As far as the east is from the west, so far does He remove our transgressions from us."* (Psalm 103:12).

I can see your loving Father removing your sins off of you and just throwing them as far away from you as possible. He goes "This is not you, it doesn't belong here; let's get rid of that."

God, Love is not keeping a record of your bad moments, He's not about to blow up in your face, He's not about to fly off the handle, He is not easily angered. There's no last straw. You're not a nuisance, you're not an annoyance, you're not an inconvenience, you're not too much. You're not walking on eggshells, you're not a frustration to Him. You're the joy set before Him. (Hebrews 12:2) You're His joy, His delight. Love can handle you. You are safe with Love. You're His beloved. He is Helper, He is available, He gives you the empowerment you need to live this life the way He designed you to. Holy Spirit is right there with you every step of the way. Living Loved is what you were born for.

ACTIVATION

Say the following out loud or within yourself...

BREAKING AGREEMENT WITH LIES:

I break the lie that I am unforgivable.
I break the lie that I am an imposter, a fraud.
I break the lie that God is easily annoyed or angered by me.

AGREEING WITH TRUTH:

I come into agreement with the truth that God likes me. He enjoys me.
I come into agreement with the truth that I am a masterpiece made by God.
I come into agreement with the truth that mistakes or failures are not the end of the world.

LOVE'S THOUGHTS TO ME TODAY:

— chapter eight —

This Is Our King.

"...Puts up with anything, Trusts God always, always looks for the best,..."
– 1 Corinthians 13:7 MSG

"Love bears up under anything and everything that comes, is ever ready to believe the best of every person,..."
– AMPC

"Love is a safe place of shelter, for it never stops believing the best for others..."
– TPT

"Love bears all things [regardless of what comes], believes all things [looking for the best in each one]," – ***AMP***

"...bears all things, believes all things,..."
– NKJV

There are many things in this world that can make us feel unsafe, exposed to danger or risk and likely to be harmed or lost. And I'm not only talking physically. Due to the days in which we are living in, facing crisis after crisis globally, not to mention personally; we can be so worn down and feel like giving up. As I write this in the middle of the COVID-19 pandemic and all the rest of the global crises that have crept up in this season, I'm aware we can feel battle-weary. We can lose faith in what God has said about us, about humanity, about His church, about His plan for the nations. We can lose trust in God, in His call on our lives and lose hope of the best outcome coming about.

I love the scripture I quoted above in various translations because it's a reminder that God, Love, is a place of shelter for you and I. Firstly, that means He knew we would have times where we face opposition or danger and need shelter. He has made Himself our designated safe place. You are not without help. You are not left to the elements as it were. In the midst of it all, you are safe in Him. This is our King. He is a safe place.

Along my adventures with God I have learnt that being a Christian, Living Loved, doesn't mean that we never go through difficult times. It doesn't mean we will never go through times of loss, waiting for a breakthrough or desperate for a miracle. Life can be really sucky at times. And I've never met anyone who enjoys going through a difficult time, facing danger or being surrounded by the opposite of "the best".

I am one person that doesn't do well with pain. I mean just watching a TV show and seeing the characters going through pain almost feels like I'm going through it myself. My husband often chuckles at how I constantly cover my face with a cushion, blanket, my hands, hide my face in his chest when painful parts come when we are watching something. What can I say? I have a high level of empathy. Sometimes we can feel like God is like that. As if He shuts His eyes, turns away, jumps ship at the first sign of danger or when the rubber really hits the road and life turns upside down. Yet the assurance here is that Love actually has the capacity to bear up under any circumstances. He can take anything. Nothing fazes God. This is our King. As the popular phrase goes, "Nothing takes Him by surprise". He doesn't leave and abandon us when it really gets hard, He is our shelter in times of trouble. Our safe place. Regardless of what comes, how the storms of life may rage, He will never leave you nor forsake you. You have a safe place in His presence. He is not missing in action. He is right there with you inviting you into His peace that surpasses all understanding. That means it's a peace that doesn't make sense, it can't be understood, it really shouldn't be present looking at the circumstances, and yet there He is, Jesus Prince of Peace in the thick of it with you (Isaiah 9:6).

"God, you're such a safe and powerful place to find refuge! You're a proven help in times of trouble—more than enough and always available whenever I need you."

– Psalms 46:1 TPT

That is who He is. He is not only our safe place but our powerful place of refuge. He is a proven help, not just a help, but He has a track record, He's got you.

"He who dwells in the shelter of the Most High Will remain secure and rest in the shadow of the Almighty [whose power no enemy can withstand]. I will say of the Lord, "He is my refuge and my fortress, My God, in whom I trust [with great confidence, and on whom I rely]!"

– Psalms 91:1-2

He is a dependable God. A constant God. He is trustworthy. If I'm being honest, one of the hardest things for me has been trusting Him after I have experienced disappointment. I know you may identify with that. Questions come of where He was, why didn't He prevent certain things from happening, why didn't He come through like He said, is He even there and on and on it goes. David went through many of these times. The Psalms are a great window to the movements of his soul and the real and raw conversations he had with God. When Jesus cried out on the cross, *"Father Father, why have you forsaken me?"*, he was actually quoting David.

As harsh a truth as it can feel, I realised I cannot reduce who God is to the level of my experience. I cannot afford to. If I do that, if I reduce my faith to the level of my disappointments, I automatically shut the door to Love's miraculous power being manifested in my life. Miracles need impossible situations in order to take place. What pleases God is faith and faith can move mountains. I have a choice to make in the face of disappointments. When life turns upside down. In those times, tears streaming down my face, fighting doubts on all fronts, my soul screaming from anguish, I have discovered a faith that cannot die somewhere deep inside me. I cannot deny His goodness. He is my safe place now and forever. He is my King. It may feel like God has abandoned me sometimes because things are so hard but the truth is that He said He will *never* leave me nor forsake me. It is not in His nature to do so. I cannot allow my feelings to be stronger than His word in my life. His word is proven, He is a shield to all who trust in Him. And when I'm struggling to believe, I remember His kindness to the man who said Lord I believe, help my unbelief and I ask for His help to believe; because He is that kind.

"And we know [with great confidence] that God [who is deeply concerned about us] causes all things to work together [as a plan] for good for those who love God, to those who are called according to His plan and purpose."
– Romans 8:28 AMP

There are mysteries in life, things we will never understand on this side of life. Things we will only understand in the light of eternity. And that's what trust is. Letting go of our right to control everything or even understand everything. That is what faith is. Trusting His nature, His goodness, who He says He is and who we have known Him to be in our lives. We get to choose this King.

We Are The Lord's

As we face life's challenges, we have the words and experiences of other followers of Jesus, those living in this world now and those who have gone to be with Him in heaven to draw strength from. As we choose to give our lives to Him and to live for Him wholeheartedly, we will face trials, spiritual, physical and emotional attacks from the enemy of our souls and persecution for the gospel. In the face of all this, Jesus gives us the confidence and assurance to be able to say that we are His like Paul said, *"If we live, we live for the Lord, and if we die, we die for the Lord. So then, whether we live or die, we are the Lord's."* (Romans 14:8 AMP). *"We are pressured in every way [hedged in], but not crushed; perplexed [unsure of finding a way out], but not driven to despair; hunted down and persecuted, but not deserted [to stand alone]; struck down, but never destroyed; always carrying around in the body the dying of Jesus, so that the [resurrection] life of Jesus also may be shown in our body."* (2 Corinthians 4:8-10 AMP).

No matter what life or the enemy throws at us, we are never deserted and we are never destroyed. We are not of this world; we are citizens of heaven. We belong to Love and can confidently say no matter what happens, we are His.

History with God

In the face of difficulties and mysteries, I am always reminded of my history with God, my testimonies, my encounters with Love, the miracles; and a new resolve rises up in me. I cannot deny who He is. I may not understand my current situation or even see a solution but I cannot deny His goodness. I cannot deny that I have tasted and seen that He is good. I know if He has come through for me before, He will do it again. He is Love, He is good and He cannot deny His nature. He will work all things, not some, not half, not a bit, but all things for good for me. That's His promise and I get to trust that. I don't know how, and sometimes it doesn't make sense. Sometimes the outcome is crushing, but as my husband often says, "We embrace Him in the mystery." As difficult as it is, I remind myself I am not after what He can do for me, I am in pursuit of Him. He is my portion, He is everything. I have often found myself echoing the sentiment of Peter in this moment, *"So Jesus said to the twelve [disciples], "You do not want to leave too, do you?" Simon Peter answered, "Lord, to whom shall we go? You [alone] have the words of eternal life [you are our only hope]."* (John 6:67-68 AMP).

Just as He asks us to believe in Him, He believes in us. Love "is ever ready to believe the best of every person". Think about it. God of the universe, creates us, gives us free will, and entrusts us with His creation, the earth, each other! He has not only entrusted us with His creation but also Himself. He has chosen to come and make His dwelling with us, mankind. Not only with us but *in us*. That is a whole lot of trust. He took the whole "I will never leave you nor forsake you" thing to another level with that one. Oh what trust He has in us! He could have chosen to live anywhere else. He could have chosen to carry out His will in another way independently from us, yet He decided He wanted to do it in relationship with you and me. He wants to use you. It is mind boggling. It is trust. And Love never stops believing the best for you. He looks for the gold in you because He placed it there.

Trusted by Love

God believes in you so much, He trusts you, He will never stop believing that you can make it. And He made sure of it by coming to live inside of you. He believes and wants the very best for you in life. He always looks for the best in you. Whatever you face in this life, you can be assured in the end you win. Jesus said, *"I have told you these things, so that in Me you may have [perfect] peace. In the world you have tribulation and distress and suffering, but be courageous [be confident, be undaunted, be filled with joy]; I have overcome the world." [My conquest is accomplished, My victory abiding.]"* (John 16:33 AMP).

His victory is abiding and it is yours. If He has conquered the world and He lives in you, you get to walk in that victory. You get to walk with this conquering King. *Love, says to you today, "Before I formed you in the womb I knew you [and approved of you as My chosen instrument], And before you were born I consecrated you [to Myself as My own]; I have appointed you as a prophet to the nations."* (Jeremiah 1:5 AMP). God created you on purpose, for purpose. You get to be His representative on earth. You are not a mistake, you are not an accident, you are not purposeless. Do not ever let the enemy convince you otherwise. Do not ever let your circumstances fool you. The enemy knows who you are and you are a danger to his kingdom; you will not be silenced. *"Yet in all these things we are more than conquerors and gain an overwhelming victory through Him who loved us [so much that He died for us]."* (Romans 8:37 AMP).

God believes in you, Love trusts you, Christ has won the victory in His resurrection and it is yours. Through it all, you are safe in His hands. Living Loved is your safe place.

ACTIVATION

Say the following out loud or within yourself...

BREAKING AGREEMENT WITH LIES:

I break the lie that I am not safe in God's hands.
I break the lie that God does not want the best for me.
I break the lie that God does not believe in me or cannot trust me.

AGREEING WITH TRUTH:

I come into agreement with the truth that I am safe in God's hands.
I come into agreement with the truth that God trusts me with Himself and His purposes.
I come into agreement with the truth that God's goodness follows me all the days of my life.

LOVE'S THOUGHTS TO ME TODAY:

— *chapter nine* —

Living Hope.

"...hopes all things [remaining steadfast during difficult times], endures all things [without weakening]."
– 1 Corinthians 13:7 AMP

"...hopes are fadeless under all circumstances, and it endures everything [without weakening]."
– AMPC

"Love never takes failure as defeat, for it never gives up."
– TPT

"...Never looks back, But keeps going to the end."
– MSG

"...hopes all things, endures all things."
– NKJV

This God who is Love remains dependable through difficult times. In fact, in the hardest times is when Love proves Himself. He proves Himself to be totally devoted to you. He is for you. Love will not weaken with time, with age, with life experience, with "withdrawals", no, He won't run out of Himself. *He is the same yesterday, today and forever* (Hebrews 13:8). He remains through difficult times, He stays. He digs His heels in and says we're going to make it baby, you're going to be ok. He is more than enough. No matter the circumstance, this God who is Love endures it all, outlives it all, out lasts it all. The pain, the hurt, the crushing, the hopelessness, the betrayal, through it all; He stays, He keeps going, right there with you, in you. He refuses to accept failure as defeat, He dares not give up on you, He endures *all* things. He is living hope.

Hope is described as the expectation of good or to trust and wait expectantly. Love's hopes are fadeless under *all* circumstances. Don't let your circumstances fool you, He won't fade. He won't go missing in action no matter how hard it gets, no matter how you feel. He never looks back; He is taking you all the way to the end. Nothing phases Love. He is never-ending hope. He is never-dying faith.

Let The Weak Say I am Strong

It is in the hard times that we learn to depend on Him more than ever before if we accept His invitation to do so. It is there that we discover the strength that is Love, *"but He has said to me, "My grace is sufficient for you [My lovingkindness and My mercy are more than enough—always available—regardless of the situation]; for [My] power is being perfected [and is completed and shows itself most effectively] in [your] weakness." Therefore, I will all the more gladly boast in my weaknesses, so that the power of Christ [may completely enfold me and] may dwell in me."* (2 Corinthians 12:9 AMP).

Paul astounds me honestly. It is no small feat to face adversity, pain, weakness, loss and choose gladness because you know that Christ's power is highlighted and He is glorified in your weakness. I've found some seasons I've been able to stand in that place with gladness well and others I have crumbled. Pain sucks. Yet there is an invitation from the Lord at our weakest points to encounter Him in a way we cannot in any other state of being. There is a surrender that is unearthed in that place. There is an authority that is birthed in that place. There is power that is experienced there that would not be otherwise. There is an eternal perspective that is clarified there. Where we remember we are citizens of another kingdom, only passing through here. Everything else is temporary but our relationship with God, that is eternal.

Let Hope Arise

Your situation is not hopeless, when you feel like giving up, He is not. He is not giving up on you, He won't change His mind about you. It doesn't matter the circumstance; God will show up. The extent of the catastrophe does not stop Him from being Love, a hiding place, a safe refuge, a Saviour, your rescue. Psalm 46 highlights this well. God, Love endures all things, no matter what they are, no matter how earth-shattering; He remains constant. He's in it for the long haul. You can have hope. You can expect good. Your future is bright. No matter what you have been or are going though, don't give up. Love is not giving up on you and neither should you.

"But the path of the just (righteous) is like the light of dawn, that shines brighter and brighter until [it reaches its full strength and glory in] the perfect day."
– Proverbs 4:18 AMP

Can you feel the brightness in your spirit? Can you feel the lightness? I can. Your future is bright in Jesus. I can feel His smile over you, I can feel His truth overshadowing you, *"The Lord your God is in your midst, a Warrior who saves. He will rejoice over you with joy; He will be quiet in His love [making no mention of your past sins], He will rejoice over you with shouts of joy."* (Zephaniah 3:17 AMP).

You are His joy; He is crazy in love with you. You make God feel and show great joy and delight so much so He shouts! He enjoys you and He is for you. He's on your side, your victorious King of Love. He is living hope and you can live in the safety of that Love. Living Loved is your place of living hope.

ACTIVATION

Say the following out loud or within yourself...

BREAKING AGREEMENT WITH LIES:

I break the lie that there is no hope for me.
I break the lie that God is distant in hard times.
I break the lie that anything could ever be bigger than God.

AGREEING WITH TRUTH:

I come into agreement with the truth that I get to live in hope.
I come into agreement with the truth that there is hope for me yet.
I come into agreement with the truth that God is dependable through difficult times.

LOVE'S THOUGHTS TO ME TODAY:

— chapter ten —

Love Never Dies.

"Love never fails [never fades out or becomes obsolete or comes to an end]..."
– 1 Corinthians 13:8 AMPC

"Love never fails [it never fades nor ends]..."
– AMP

"Love never stops loving..."
– TPT

"Love never fails..."
– NKJV

"Love never dies..."
– MSG

Love never dies. They tried to kill Him over 2000 years ago and yet He rose again on the third day. He just won't die. He just can't be extinguished. And He is for you, *yes you*. All of that extravagant, never ending, never dying Love is focused on you. That's the truth. Love never stops loving. God never stops loving. It's His nature and He cannot deny His nature. He can't help but to love. He can't help but to love you. He *is* love. He is big enough; never runs out; never ends and He'll never run out on you. He is more than enough. He is and there is nothing that can unmake Him. I've said it before and I'll say it again; He loves you, because He loves you, because He loves you; because He is love. Your relationship with Him is not based on your works but on His nature and His nature is steadfast love. Love will *never* stop loving you. He will never stop being Love. It is who He is. And He is sure about you.

You're a Dream

Love dreamt you. You are God's dream come true. Truly. You are God's dream wrapped in flesh. An expression of God on earth. A masterpiece, signed by Love Himself. He won't leave, desert or abandon you. He won't give up on you. He won't fail. He is besotted with you. He adores you. He was intentional about making you and He is intentional about you now. David knew this all too well, he said *"I thank you, God, for making me so mysteriously complex! Everything you do is marvelously breathtaking. It simply amazes me to think about it! How thoroughly you know me, Lord! You formed my innermost being, shaping my delicate inside and my intricate outside, and wove them all together in my mother's womb."* (Psalms 139:13-14 TPT).

The truth is that you are mysteriously complex, marvelously breathtaking and thoroughly known. That's how God made you! He was always speaking of how lovely you are from the start, from the very beginning. You are breathtaking.

Nowhere to go but Love

> *"Where could I go from Your Spirit? Where could I run and hide from your face? If I go up to heaven, You're there! If I go down to the realm of the dead, You're there too! If I fly with wings into the shining dawn, You're there! If I fly into the radiant sunset, You're*

there waiting! Wherever I go, Your hand will guide me; Your strength will empower me. It's impossible to disappear from You or to ask the darkness to hide me, for Your presence is everywhere, bringing light into my night.'

– Psalms 139:7-11

Love is stronger, brighter, more powerful than anything else. He is bigger than it all. You cannot outrun Him. You cannot hide from Him; you cannot repel Him. Nothing can. Love chooses you and all He wants is for you to choose Him back. Love chose you and won't ever let you go (John 10:16-18). Love gave Himself willingly just for you, for relationship with you. To be with you for eternity. You are the desire of heaven. You are Love's desire. There is a longing in the heart of the God of the universe that only you can meet.

"For He has said, "I will never [under any circumstances] desert you [nor give you up nor leave you without support, nor will I in any degree leave you helpless], nor will I forsake or let you down or relax My hold on you [assuredly not]!" So we take comfort and are encouraged and confidently say, "The Lord is my Helper [in time of need], I will not be afraid. What will man do to me?"

– Hebrews 13:5-6 AMP

This is who Love is. This is what He is like. As we walk with Him, enjoy Him, find our sustenance in Him, make Him our source of everything, He promises that we are His and He is ours. He won't desert you, He doesn't know how; He is Love.

Love committed to be with us to the end. Jesus said this to the disciples and I believe it applies to us His disciples in the now, *"I am with you always [remaining with you perpetually - regardless of circumstance, and on every occasion], even to the end of the age."* (Matthew 28:20 AMP). What comfort it is to know that Love will never come to an end. Other things may end but He will not. He will be with us to the end and always, beyond the end of life on earth. He is infinite Love; He is eternal Love.

No thing can Separate You

He will never let anything separate you from Himself. Nothing can separate you from Love. Let that sink in. Nothing. *No thing.* Not a single thing can separate you from God's love. Nothing is more powerful than Him. Love chose you and it's forever. It's a done deal and nothing can change that. Love sees you. Love knows you. Love chooses you. Every single day, He chooses you. He surrounds you. He loves you. He is cheering you on. This is the truth. Love chose you. Nothing can ever change that.

> *"For God has proved His love by giving us His greatest treasure, the gift of His Son. And since God freely offered Him up as the sacrifice for us all, He certainly won't withhold from us anything else He has to give. So, what does all this mean? If God has determined to stand with us, tell me, who then could ever stand against us? Who then would dare to accuse those whom God has chosen in love to be His? God Himself is the judge who has issued His final verdict over them—"Not guilty!" Who then is left to condemn us? Certainly not Jesus, the Anointed One! For He gave His life for us, and even more than that, He has conquered death*

and is now risen, exalted, and enthroned by God at His right hand. So how could He possibly condemn us since He is continually praying for our triumph? Who could ever divorce us from the endless love of God's Anointed One? Absolutely no one! For nothing in the universe has the power to diminish His love toward us. Troubles, pressures, and problems are unable to come between us and heaven's love. What about persecutions, deprivations, dangers, and death threats? No, for they are all impotent to hinder omnipotent love,"

– Romans 8:31-35 TPT

He is all powerful Love; He overcame it all just to have you. Love never dies.

One of the greatest acts of worship is to let Him love you. Let Love be who He is in your life. Believe Him. When we live loved, we become unstoppable.

You get to live in the reality of this attribute of God's nature. God is Love. Living loved is for you.

Living Loved.

ACTIVATION

Say the following out loud or within yourself...

BREAKING AGREEMENT WITH LIES:

I break agreement with the lie that love could end.
I break agreement with the lie that Love could stop loving me.
I break agreement with the lie that there is a limit to how much of Love I can experience.

AGREEING WITH TRUTH:

I come into agreement with the truth that Love chooses me.
I come into agreement with the truth that Love will never stop loving me.
I come into agreement with the truth that Love will be with me always and forever.
I receive you Love and I choose to Live Loved.

LOVE'S THOUGHTS TO ME TODAY:

Acknowledgements

Steffany Gretzinger, your encounters with Love shared with the world through melodies have changed my life. Thank you for not being too afraid to come out of hiding and allowing Love to use you to hand me the invitation to come out of hiding too. "And as the dawn breaks, and the clouds clear, in an open space, together we will run. And oh as we run, what hindered Love will only become part of the story."

Thank you to all those who created spaces for me to simply encounter Love along my adventures with Daddy God. To the Key family, Torquay friends, Rediscover Church Exeter, UK family, Bethel Church Redding, CA, USA family, the TePaske family, the Hesmert family, Jerry Coughlin, and many more who have trusted and supported me as a sent one, thank you from the bottom of my heart.

Thank you to Hannah Bvumbura and Danielle Jooste for the hours spent processing, encountering His joy, belly laughing, ugly crying, breaking lies and encountering Love together. Thank you for going on this crazy adventure of following the steps Love gave me with me and still being here years later, through the highs and lows. You're my day ones.

Thank you to my parents for handing me the true gospel, it set a little girl's soul on fire so much that I could never stop burning for Jesus. Your hunger for Him has caused me to live my life in pursuit of authentic encounters with the Living God. My highest calling is intimacy with Him and I cannot be satisfied with anything less than what God made available to us through the cross. Thank you for showing me how to love

Jesus wholeheartedly, through it all. Thank you for teaching me that He is worthy of it all.

Dylan, my best friend, my scrumptious husband. You had me when you began to pour your love in words over me and they felt so familiar because they were what Daddy God says to me. You took truth right out of His mouth and spoke it to my heart and that's when I knew you were the love of my life. Thank you for living to love me like Christ loves the Church. Thank you for believing in me. Thank you for challenging me to live loved by going after all that is possible in Him. Thank you for instilling in me the undying belief that there is more, practically, wholly. We get to dream big and never stop. Nothing is impossible. You are faith personified. Thank you for being you. I love you.

Daddy God, Jesus, Holy Spirit; words are not enough. Thank You for choosing me, for revealing Yourself to me as Love. For healing and continuing to heal that scared little girl's heart, inviting me to come out of hiding, for the Love bubble, inviting me to follow the signs You gave me and to live like the Love I experienced in the secret place is real, because You are.

Thank you for inviting me to run like there's nothing You wouldn't do for me. I trust You with my heart things, in the good times and the hard times, now and forever. Thank You for seeing me. Intimacy with You is my highest calling. I give You my Hineni once again. Here I am, send me. All for Your glory. You are worthy of it all.

I love You.

About The Author

Nqo Mafukidze is an international speaker, worshiper and author who has been in ministry for 20 years. As an itinerant Pastor, she travels the nations preaching and seeing God heal hearts with His love, save, heal bodies and bring freedom to people. Intimacy with God is her highest calling. Her passion is seeing people encounter God as Love, this revelation and encounters that have followed have changed her life. Nqo loves to help people encounter the nature of God as Love and then live like that Love is real; because He is. She calls this Living Loved.

Born in Zimbabwe and raised in England, she has a degree in Accounting and Finance from Exeter University, UK. She is also a graduate of Bethel School of Supernatural Ministry located at Bethel Church in Redding, California, USA.

She is married to her best friend, Dylan Mafukidze and together they burn to see revival, reformation and renaissance in the nations.